Jdxie,
      We did not know
what you needed.
      But I know what
everyone has. - troubles,
trials, and tribulations.
      Thus we bought
you the solution to
all three. A little
book in which one
can always find God —
      The Resolver of all
              troubles.

                    Linda

# God Is Everywhere

# God Is Everywhere

By Barbara Burrow

Illustrated by

Mary Hamilton

♔

Hallmark Editions

# God Is Everywhere

If you've ever wondered

where God lives . . .

If sometimes he seems far away

in his house in heaven,

look around you . . .

God is everywhere.

You see his face

in a woodland flower.

You feel his touch

in the gentle rain.

You hear his voice

in the murmuring winds.

*Even in small secret places,*

*he is always near.*

His miracles are as small

as a snowflake . . .

*and as great as*

*a sky full of stars.*

God brings the spirit of joy

to your home . . .

and the spirit of peace

and thanksgiving

where you worship.

When you speak to God,

He guides you.

He is your strength

when things don't go right . . .

And your comfort

when you are

lonely or sad.

When you are kind and thoughtful,

you are helping to do God's work . . .

and in return

He sends you the gift

of happiness.

God is in every one of us.

He is in our friends who like us

just the way we are.

He is in our parents who help us grow up and love us always.

*God is in those*

*who think and act as we do . . .*

and in those who

may be different.

*God is love, and he lives*

*everywhere there is love.*

Most of all, God lives in your heart.